"This collection of 100 prayers by a Catholic priest and a Jewish journalist was composed for use in churches and synagogues as well as privately. This fills a much-needed void of prayers for any occasion when Jews and Christians come together. All congregational libraries should consider this a 'must' purchase."

Church and Synagogue Libraries

"This beautifully composed volume of prayers, suitable for every occasion when Jews and Christians are together, is long overdue. It serves well, moreover, as a reminder that the Jewish-Christian enterprise that has flowered in our time is not only a matter of 'dialogue' and cooperative social action but also an occasion for two related faith-traditions to meet in the spirit—in prayer."

Rev. Edward Flannery
author of *Anguish of the Jews*

"The authors, one Jewish and one Christian, combine the spiritualities of their traditions, offering this collection of private, devotional prayers, dialogical in style, ecumenical in nature, drawn from varied facets of ordinary life. These prayers 'bring Christians and Jews together in God and toward God.' Simplicity and gracefulness of expression mark their aptness for all readers and all occasions."

Books & Religion

"Have you ever been invited to give a blessing at a public occasion? Are you asked to be denominationally inclusive in your prayer? Does your individual prayer life need words to describe your current thoughts of pain, thanksgiving, or praise of God? If so, this is the text for you!"

Catholic Campus Ministry Newsletter

"This book is for those who have had feelings that can't be put into words. The authors take some of the most magical and some of the most mundane human experiences and put them into beautiful prayers. There are prayers for everything imaginable."

The Catholic Observer

"A Jewish journalist and a Roman catholic priest in Brazil have prepared these 100 prayers....Most are a page in length, intended for use on a variety of occasions. They echo the richness of the Scriptures, and are based on the Judeo-Christian tradition of love and respect for the one God and for other people, and concern for earth and all creation. This book will be helpful in personal prayer, in classrooms, and in small groups. Recommended."

National (Canada) Bulletin on Liturgy

"I am happy to discover a collection of very fine prayers and blessings suitable for all sorts of occasions when Christian and Jews gather. I am pleased to recommend this book."

Dr. Richard Lux
Sacred Heart School of Theology

"These prayers are biblical and touch every aspect of worship and human life. Overwhelmingly the authors communicate a sense of praise to the God who calls us into being and to covenant and mutual respect, whose power shields us in every age and whose presence we encounter every day."

Theodolite

"These prayers on varied subjects have a kind of universal human appeal...."

Liguorian

"These prayers are a dialogue between traditions....Most of them are written in the first person singular, but they can be adapted to the first person plural for communal prayer."

Celebration

Prayers
of Blessing
and Praise
for All Occasions

Hugo Schlesinger

Humberto Porto

TWENTY-THIRD PUBLICATIONS

Mystic, Connecticut

Rev. Porto and Dr. Schlesinger have also published (in Brazil) the following titles:

Trilogy of Interreligious Dialogue

> Popes and Jews
> Anatomy of Anti-Semitism
> Jesus Was a Jew

The Religious Culture Library (5 volumes)

> Religions: Past and Present
> Beliefs, Sects, and Religious Symbols
> Religious Thought and Messages
> World Religious Leaders
> World Geography of Religions

Prayers of Blessing and Praise for All Occasions was translated from the Portuguese by Michel Leipziger.

Third printing 1989

Twenty-Third Publications
185 Willow Street
P.O. Box 180
Mystic, CT 06355

ISBN 0-89622-311-6
Library of Congress Catalog Card Number 86-51259

Foreword

Christians worship not just any God, but quite specifically the One God, the God of Israel. This was emphasized most powerfully by Pope John Paul II's recent - and deeply prayerful - visit to the Great Synagogue in Rome. The Pope's gesture was not simply a neighborly visit but a true spiritual pilgrimage. Christian prayer, the Pope's visit affirms, finds its source, structure, and inspiration not just in any prayer, but quite specifically in Jewish prayer, the prayer of biblical Israel (e.g. the Psalms) and the prayer of the synagogue (e.g. the Our Father and even the eucharistic celebration itself). Therefore, from the Christian perspective, it is proper to pray together with Jews to the One God, to whom both religious traditions give continual faithful witness. As the recent "guidelines for Catholic-Jewish Relations" of the Secretariat for Catholic-Jewish Relations of the National Conference of Catholic Bishops state: ·

> Prayer in common with Jews should, when mutually accep-
> table, be encouraged, especially in matters of common con-
> cern, such as peace and the welfare of the community. Such
> prayer should meet the spiritual sensibilities of both parties,
> finding its inspiration in our common faith in the One God
> (USCC Publication no. 966).

It needs also to be acknowledged that the "spiritual sensibilities" referred to here are not minor, but major concerns for both communities. While both Christianity and rabbinic Judaism find their source in biblical Israel and its Torah, two thousand years of separate (if connected) religious development and an often tragic history of Christian persecution of Jews separate us, even as the One God who called us both into being as religious communities binds us together in covenant.

It cannot be presumed, therefore, that Christians and Jews will enter into the act of prayer at precisely the same point. An authentic context of true dialogue, with all that implies (see the 1975 Vatican Guidelines, for example), needs to be established. Prayer, our dialogue with God, is the most intimate activity in which we humans can engage. That intimacy, and its necessary freedom and autonomy, must at all times be respected.

In approaching the remarkably moving and sensitive prayers contained in this book, one must distinguish between what we Catholics would call "private" or devotional prayer and "public" or communal prayer. The latter, in Catholic perspectives, forms the formal worship of the church as such. Christian prayer that is not part of the official liturgical cycle, even when done in groups, falls into the former category, as do all of the prayers here presented. Hence, and this must be emphasized, there is no desire for or danger of "syncretism," or blurring the lines between our two distinct traditions in what follows. The prayers, composed in the spirit of dialogue, reflect that spirit, and while celebrating what Jews and Christians share (which is far more than most of us, over the centuries, have been willing to acknowledge), their context and content scrupulously preserve those areas where our faith-traditions differ, as must those who use them.

All biblical prayer is bounded by the horizons of creation and redemption, celebrating the Creator and yearning for the redemption of history. Jews and Christians in prayer, then, meet in a comparable hope founded on the same promise made to Abraham by the One God who is the Master of history (Gn 12:1-3); Heb 6:13-18). In the dialogical context, Christians especially need to base their prayer on the humility of their hope for the coming of God's reign, a coming which, while ensured and mysteriously present, is manifestly "not yet" in history, as Christians pray in the Our Father: "Thy Kingdom come."

The prayers that follow avoid, as I believe is prudent, direct expression of the messianic longing which infuses the prayer-traditions of each of our communities, though in highly distinctive ways. Yet a sense of that longing, and of that eschatological hope, one may say, unconsciously permeates these moving offerings. This is in a sense inescapable, since the eschatological dimension is central to both Jewish and Christian spirituality. Carefully and properly understood, this fact should be for both a matter of profound encouragement. As the 1985 Vatican "Notes on the Correct Presentation of Jews and Judaism in Preaching and Catechesis" state:

> In underlining the eschatological dimension of Christianity, we shall reach a greater awareness that the people of God of the Ancient and the New Testament are tending toward a like end in the future: the coming or return of the Messiah—even if they start from two different points of view (USCC Publications, no. 970).

The dialogical prayers here presented, it is my conviction, will not only deeply enrich Christian spirituality, but will serve in doing so as a living reminder of the greater tasks that we are called to do as Jews and Christians today. Again in the words of the "Notes":

Attentive to the same God who has spoken, hanging on the same word, we have to witness to one same memory and one common hope in Him who is the master of history. We must also accept our responsibility to prepare the world for the coming of the Messiah by working together for social justice, respect for the rights of persons and nations, and for social and international reconciliation. To this we are driven, Jews and Christians, by the command to love our neighbor, by a common hope for the Kingdom of God, and by the great heritage of the Prophets.

Dr. Eugene J. Fisher
Secretariat for Catholic-Jewish Relations
National Council of Catholic Bishops

Foreword

Prayer starts within the person. It is a bridge from the human heart to God, whose call changes that heart. Prayer is daily action in word and gesture, continuing a relationship rooted in the very beginning of creation: person and God, community and God, in fraternity and peace. Prayer renews spiritual life as well as the experience of God's presence. The word of praise celebrating God reinforces our inner life in the midst of the world's turmoil and unending noise. Prayer introduces the peace of inward silence, the stillness of God's communion.

Prayer overcomes loneliness, placing a person in a community of shared song and smybols, achieving the companionship of the soul and a sense of loving relationships. Prayer is a full fellowship of the heart, an open window to others, and to the Other, the Eternal.

Prayer joins people of the same faith. It should also be a bond of intimacy with believers of different religions. This is a hope rarely achieved, though of paramount significance for committed, religious people. The common belief in God unites Christians and Jews, although confrontation and misunderstanding have plagued the relationship, with sad consequences for the Jewish people. There have been centuries of persecution and suffering, contempt and pain. It is my hope, my prayer, that those times are forever past. For everything its season, and now there is a time to share spirituality and silence, a time to offer reconciliation and friendship. Such a time is a time of prayer, of celebrating God's Word, reciting texts that echo God's command to love and respect each other. It is a time of joy and renewal for Christians and Jews.

The present selection of prayers was prepared for joint Christian-Jewish recital of prayers entailing fervor and spirituality. The authors, Hugo Schlesinger and Humberto Porto, composed them in Brazil, in Portuguese. Both authors are active in the interfaith dialogue in their country and have pioneered joint publications on the New Testament and the history of Christianity and Judaism through the centuries. They are aware of the problems related to joint prayer, aware of Jewish sensibilities and the danger of syncretism. But they convey in their prayers a sense of religiousness and spirituality covering every aspect of life. The prayers are described as dialogues of faith, personal realization, loneliness, and meaning for those who suffer or are sick or hungry. They touch every aspect of human life, dreams and realities, hopes and desires. They also show concern for life, for God's presence in every human being and all that exists in the universe.

The prayers in this volume are an act of recognition acknowledging that we are all children of one God. They are also an act of faith and hope in human destiny. The prayers bring Christians and Jews together in God and toward God. The authors accomplish this with a sense of gratitude echoing the thanksgiving hymn of the synagogue prayer:

> Gratefully we acknowledge that you are the Lord our God and God of all people, the God of all Generations. You are the rock of our life, the Power that shields us in every age. We thank You and sing Your praises: for our lives, which are in Your hands; for our souls, which are in Your keeping; for the signs of your Presence we encounter everyday; and for Your wondrous gifts at all times, morning, noon and night.

Let us pray together.

Rabbi Leon Klenicki
Anti-Defamation League
of B'nai B'rith

Contents

Foreword by Dr. Eugene J. Fisher   *v*
Foreword by Rabbi Leon Klenicki   *ix*

Morning Prayer   1
Evening Prayer   2
Prayer Before Work   3
Prayer Before a Meeting   4
Prayer After a Meeting   5
Prayer Before a Meal   6
Prayer After a Meal   7
Daily Prayer   8
Prayer Before a Journey   9
Prayer on Returning From Vacation   10
Prayer on a Day of Rest   11
Prayer on a Festive Day   12
Prayer on a Birthday   13
Prayer at the Start of a New Year   14
Prayer at the End of the Year   16

Prayer to the Creator   17
Prayer of Adoration   18
Prayer of Praise   19
Prayer on Contemplating Nature   20
Prayer in the Divine Presence   21
Prayer at a Silent Moment   22
Prayer for Full Life   23
Prayer for Faith in Time of Doubt   24
Prayer for Perseverance   26
Prayer to God Within   27
Prayer to Recognize the Signs of God   28
Prayer for Uprightness   29
Prayer for Spiritual Concentration   30

Prayer for Spiritual Guidance   31
Prayer to Love in Deed   32
Prayer of Praise for the Gift of Life   33

Prayer for a Mother   34
Prayer for a Father   35
Prayer for One's Children   36
A Husband's Prayer   37
A Wife's Prayer   38
A Pregnant Woman's Prayer   39
Prayer for the Sake of Children   40
A Youngster's Prayer   41
Prayer for the Elderly   42
A Sick Person's Prayer   43
A Teacher's Prayer   44
A Physician's Prayer   45
An Executive's Prayer   46
A Worker's Prayer   47
A Driver's Prayer   48

Prayer for Courage   49
Prayer for Faith   50
Prayer for Protection   52
Prayer of Thanksgiving   53
Prayer for Divine Grace   54
Prayer for Patience   55
Prayer to Use Time Well   56
Prayer for Personal Achievement   57
Prayer for Happiness   58
Prayer Before an Important Decision   59
Prayer for a Sincere Life   60
Prayer After Success   61
Prayer After Failure   62
Prayer During Loneliness   63
Prayer for Repentance   64
Prayer to Resist Violence   65
Prayer to Preserve Mental Balance   66
Prayer Before a Test   67
Prayer to Calm the Spirit   68
Prayer to Discover the Meaning of Life   69

Prayer for the Suffering   70
Prayer for the Poor   71
Prayer for the Hungry   72
Prayer for the Sick   73
Prayer for the Dying   74
Prayer for the Dead   75
Prayer for Mourners   76
Prayer for Orphans   77
Prayer for Catastrophe Victims   78
Prayer for Refugees   79
Prayer for Prisoners   80
Prayer for Victims of Injustice   81

Prayer to Work for Goodness   82
Prayer at Harvest Time   83
Prayer to Humanize Life   84
Prayer for the Spread of Truth   85
Prayer for the City   86
Prayer for a Community   87
Prayer for the Progress of Science   88
Prayer for the Development of Culture   89
Prayer for International Harmony   90
Prayer for Our Country   91
Prayer for Security   92
Prayer for Rulers   93
Prayer for Religious Leaders   94
Prayer for Peace   95

Prayer of Those Seeking God   96
Prayer for Unity   97
Prayer of Thanks for Friends   98
Prayer for Sharing   99
Prayer for Fellowship   100
Prayer for Reverence for the Bible   101
Prayer for Religious Dialogue   102
Prayer for the World's Salvation   104

Index of Prayers   109

PRAYERS OF BLESSING AND PRAISE

FOR ALL OCCASIONS

Morning Prayer

From behind the clouds the morning sun appears,
  and light begins to shine on a new day.
God of the Covenant, I am glad to be able to start,
  today, a new task,
  to start all over again, in health and good spirits.
I bless you, my God, for the great will to live,
  and because you accompany me, guide me,
  direct my steps, and give me faith.
I am grateful to you for the miracles
  we discover at each moment
  that help us to live
  and to use the works of your creation.
Praised be you, my Lord,
  for this new day that is born.
Give me your help and guidance.
Guide me with your inspiration,
  benevolence, and blessing.
Help me to fulfill my duties,
  and to achieve my aims.
May your light, the divine light, continue
  to shine upon me.
May this new day be for me
  and for everyone
  another day of your glory
  and a day of peace and happiness.
Amen.

Evening Prayer

*A*nother day ends and the lights go out.
Night testifies to the greatness of your creation.
Blessed are you, Father of the Universe,
    for the curiosity you awakened in me,
    for the daring plans,
    for the will power,
    and for the light that shone on my ways.
Blessed are you, King of the Universe,
    guide of those who worship you
    and place in you their trust
    and unwavering faith in the destiny
    that you hold in store for us.
Today, as always, I thank you,
    my Father, my Lord and Creator of the Universe,
    for another day of struggle and accomplishments,
    for the difficult hours and passing worries.
Blessed are you, Lord and Protector,
    who has lit our ways
    and kept us courageous,
    who has given us another opportunity
    to close with credit the balance sheet of this day.
The stars remind us of your infinite power,
    and the quietness of the night
    witnesses to the majesty of your silence.
Amen.

Prayer Before Work

Eternal Lord, you have created work
    so that we can value our lives.
Through work you give each one of us the opportunity
    to learn to overcome obstacles
    and to feel the taste of accomplishment.
Work has become a sentinel to virtue,
    making it possible
    to have peace, health, abundance, and ease.
We are privileged because you stand by, Lord,
    with your positive and encouraging inspiration.
With the good disposition you offer us,
    we discover through our work the joy of living.
Lord, you gave us this spice of life
    and the opportunity to serve your purposes.
Without work, we do not experience satisfaction
    nor receive valuable rewards.
Thanks to you, Lord, we know how to work
    and to put our imprint on the world for useful changes.
Without work, life seems to be a ship
    adrift at sea.
With work, we are leaders and captains of our lives.
Thank you, Lord, for the grace
    of being able to begin and to accomplish,
    as well as we can,
    all our tasks.
Amen.

Prayer Before a Meeting

Light of truth and of kindness,
    my Lord and my God,
    I cannot start the proceedings of this meeting
    without directing to you
    my call and praise.
I call for your guidance
    so that you direct us from beginning to end
    and help us reach with joy the best results.
Praise to your presence.
I call upon you to preside over and direct
    the best of our concerns and thoughts.
Universal Mother, give us the opportunity
    to gain from this meeting
    increased unity and friendship.
Under your parental gaze, always watchful,
    we ask you to bless our ideas
    and the projects we put into action.
May all we do here develop safely
    for the greater glory of your name
    and for our true benefit and use.
Bless abundantly, God,
    all who are present
    and all the tasks we will accomplish.
Amen.

Prayer After a Meeting

Accept, O Father, my gratitude
and the thanks of those who joined me
in this meeting's proceedings.
During the time we were together
we tried to remain under the influence
of your spirit.
O Father, more than once we could feel in our midst
the power of your presence
and of your love.
All the plans and projects we sketched here
are entrusted to your blessing.
Without your constant protection, O Father,
nothing can be accomplished.
Continue to help us with your loving kindness
so that we may serve you
and glorify you in all endeavors.
We continually thank you, Father,
for the positive results of our meeting.
Amen.

Prayer Before a Meal

Blessed are you, O Lord, our God;
    you make our bread spring forth from the earth
    and transform the bounty of nature
    into food that sustains our life.
Blessed are you, King of the Universe;
    you grant us life to be used for the benefit of others,
    and food according to our needs,
    protecting us and shielding us from hunger.
In this rich world,
    which is at the same time so full of poverty,
    the bread you give us is one more gift
    for which we humbly thank you,
    glorifying your name among your children.
We ask you, O God, Creator of all human beings,
    that this nourishment you offer us
    should not be lacking to any of your children,
    filling all human needs.
Blessed are you, O Eternal One, our God;
    you sustain us day after day,
    freeing us from hunger and thirst
    and manifesting your majesty
    to all of us, your children.
Amen.

Prayer After a Meal

How wonderful, Eternal Lord of All,
    to be neither hungry nor thirsty,
    to feel relaxed, satisfied, and happy.
How wonderful not to be jealous of others
    and to enjoy the fruit of our labor.
How wonderful to sit at table,
    to eat and drink,
    to enjoy the bounty and beauty of life.
How wonderful to have health and to be able to savor
    the food that preserves our health.
How wonderful to be able to lift our eyes
    to thank you, our Father, for all these gifts.
Blessed are you,
    Creator of all riches;
    you give us the joy of thanking you.
Blessed are you, Lord of the Universe,
    who has privileged us
    to sit at a table of plenty,
    a table set by your will.
Praised are you, God, our Protector,
    for the nourishment,
    fruits of the earth,
    created and planned by your kindness.
Praised are you, our Father,
    for all the good things you give us
    to share with others:
    bread, love, and happiness.
Amen.

Daily Prayer

Lord All-powerful, I pray you for daily bread,
    a safe roof,
    the necessary health,
    a day without accidents,
    and a quiet night.
Grant me the vigor
    to endure the worries and tribulations
    that emerge from life's vicissitudes.
Lord, preserve today and always
    the light of my eyes,
    the use of my intelligence and senses.
I pray, do not close my heart
    to human feelings,
    nor cross my arms
    when faced with the demands of human love.
Lord, keep away from my path
    the pitfalls of injustice and slander.
By your grace, I will set my mind to live in peace
    with everyone,
    to respect their customs,
    their right to express opinions, to disagree,
    and to defend themselves.
I will, in your name, cultivate
    the unity of my family,
    the good will of my neighbors and my colleagues,
    the faithfulness of my friends,
    and peace toward all.
Lord, I beg your blessing
    for each hour of my day
    and for all the days of my life.
Amen.

Prayer Before a Journey

Lord our God, before you there are no secrets;
   nothing is hidden from your eyes
   and nothing happens without your permission.
Grant me the happiness of beginning this trip
   entrusted to you;
   permit me to go and to return in peace and tranquillity,
   in your infinite love and mercy.
Accompany me with your loving security
   and direct my footsteps
   with the steady love of your heart,
   keeping me always close to you, Lord.
May I see clearly the obstacles
   of my journey,
   and may I keep safe from affliction and despair,
   thanks to your blessing and care.
Blessed are you, O Eternal God;
   you have protected me in such a way
   that by the light of your presence
   I shall always find new roads
   and fulfilling answers to my yearnings.
Amen.

Prayer on Returning From Vacation

Eternal Father, I thank you for the days of rest
    which I was permitted to enjoy;
    they were truly healthy
    for my body and for my mind.
How shall I express my gratitude
    for this precious and fruitful opportunity?
Eternal Father, I praise you for the sky and the sun,
    for the water and the trees, which express for me
    the beauty of the world you created.
I praise you for the kind hearts I met,
    who extended unending favors to me during my trip.
I praise you for the smiling faces
    that relaxed me,
    and left me reconciled
    with the joy of living.
I praise you and thank you, Eternal Father,
    because I returned home healthy and safe.
Now restored, I undertake my duties again,
    having known the pleasant and happy experiences
    I had during my vacation.
I thank you for everything,
    now and always.
Amen.

Prayer on a Day of Rest

Blessed are you, Lord,
    for the relaxation of this day,
    which is consecrated to you.
I join all human beings
    who serve you with reverence and love,
    and glorify you by honest and good deeds.
Blessed are you, Lord,
    because today you let me restore
    my strength
    for the daily work
    that dignifies my life
    and extends your creative work.
Blessed are you, Lord,
    for the opportunity to have another day
    to spend with my family and friends;
    they are part of my life,
    and I entrust them to your care.
Blessed are you, Lord,
    for the well-being of this quiet day,
    which permits me to gratefully regain
    the enthusiasm and the joy of living.
Blessed are you, Lord,
    because you today restore my spirit
    so that I can always walk
    in your light
    and be accompanied by your caring presence.
Amen.

Prayer on a Festive Day

So much gladness and contentment
fill my heart, O Divine Lord!
I would like to sing and laugh
and shout my feelings.
My heart pounds in excitement
for the meaning of this day.
Now is the moment
to express my praise to you.
I want to thank you, my Lord,
for this festive hour and for this happy day.
I am grateful to you
for your presence and love,
for your understanding and care.
Thank you for this special holiday,
for the possibility to dream
with open eyes.
I stand in your presence, Lord
to say thank you
for this day
and for the happiness it brings.
Amen.

Prayer on a Birthday

As I celebrate my birthday today,
    permit me, God,
        to celebrate it with you in this private way,
        opening my heart to you.
If I reached this year
    it is because of you,
        who were never absent from my life.
Your presence has given me the will
    to fight against what is selfish and evil.
You have accompanied me, Lord,
    with the power of your kindness
    all along the journey of my life;
    you have preserved me
    with a strong and happy disposition to do your will.
Make me happy,
    this never fully-grown child,
    by granting me the gift of your peace and protection.
Remove from me
    all shadow of restlessness and anxiety.
Keep from me all feelings
    that are alien to your spirit and your law.
Make all my remaining days productive;
    may they shine in their concern for others.
Keep lit for many years, O God,
    the spark of my life,
    so that I may thank you daily
    for the light of your blessing.
Amen.

Prayer at the Start of a New Year

In the beginning of this New Year,
  when a new page is inscribed in the Book of Life,
  I invoke you, my Father and Mother,
  and I beg you,
  with confident and humble spirit,
  the grace of being able to dedicate my life
  to silent good deeds.
Grant me the ability to see, hear, and feel,
  the freedom to think, speak, and act.
Fulfill my everyday needs
  and direct my steps on the path of life.
Father and Mother of the Universe,
  I beg your justice
  for all people, in every corner of this world,
  and a little peace and tranquillity for me,
  thus preserving confidence and faith in my heart.
You, Eternal God, who crown the sky with stars
  and conduct the planets in their paths,
  enlighten the sages,
  give vision to the scientists,
  and fill my days with light and love.
You know, God, who will live
  and who will die this year,
  who will remain at peace,
  who will engage in violence,
  who will remain poor
  and who will stay rich,
  who will be fed
  and who will hunger.

Look upon us with the full measure
    of your grace and blessing.
Our God, God of our ancestors,
    you rule the skies and govern the earth;
    may my repentance, prayer, and supplication
    pierce the sound pollution of the world
    and reach your ears.
May my sincere words be lifted to your presence
    so that you may bless me in this New Year,
    with your glory, justice, and peace,
    in your eternal kingdom
    that knows no frontiers.
Amen.

Prayer at the End of the Year

In the twilight of this year
    that is about to end, O Lord, God,
    hear my voice and supplication.
My heart tries to express my gratitude
    for all the benefits I received.
I am grateful, Lord,
    for every moment of my life,
    for your kindness and support,
    for the light and happiness in our homes,
    and for the strength and energy
     with which you have endowed me.
This year I endured difficult and sad hours,
    but you have cheered me in my affliction and sadness.
Many tears ran down my face,
    but you taught me
    to understand the holy designs of life.
With great humility, I turn my face to you, my Lord.
Give me strength to serve you with all my heart;
    make me more prudent, more charitable,
    more steadfast in faith.
Help me to find the wisdom
    that will guide me through life.
You are the source of richness, of life and light.
Bless me and all your human family.
Grant to those who call upon you, Lord,
    liberty, justice, and peace—
    grant this to all your children.
Amen.

Prayer to the Creator

Blessed are you, Creator of the Universe,
  who out of darkness brought forth light
  and who rule the universe by your word.
Send far away from us
  the darkness of error and evil
  and direct us to the knowledge of your name's glory.
Blessed are you, Creator of the Universe,
  who brought forth from nothing
  everything
  and renew unceasingly days and seasons.
Be merciful with us in your great power
  and multiply in us the grace of your kindness.
Blessed are you, Creator of the Universe,
  who created human beings with amazing perfection
  and who want your image and likeness to shine in them.
Accept us all under your shining gaze
  and grant that we may live up to your aim of love.
Blessed are you, Creator of the Universe,
  who sustain all beings in time and space
  and penetrate everything
  with your overpowering presence.
Fulfill the innermost desires of your heart
  and guide in peace
  the destiny of all human beings.
Blessed are you, Creator of the Universe,
  who communicate your energy to all created beings
  and direct humankind in your path.
Make us your co-workers in the harmony of the world,
  and help us to fulfill in history
  the mystery of your creation.
Amen.

Prayer of Adoration

No matter how high my thought flies,
    I touch only the edge of your mystery.
Highest and Eternal Lord,
    you inhabit a region of unreachable light.
I worship you in your luminous mystery.
Only a suggestion of your divine Being
    is given to us in life.
Highest and Eternal Lord,
    you live beyond everything that exists.
I worship you and praise you in your infinity.
Truth and mysterious footprints
    reveal you in human history.
Highest and Eternal Lord,
    you free me for my complete surrender to love.
I worship you in your freeing mystery.
Because you are transcendent,
    you embrace everything
    and never remain far from life.
Highest and Eternal Lord,
    you neither frighten me,
    nor keep me far from you.
I worship you in your inviting and involving mystery.
Amen.

Prayer of Praise

Glorious and Eternal Father,
  all creation sings your praise.
Whatever exists belongs to you.
You are the only, the one Lord.
Eternal Father,
  this heart of flesh
  turns to you in confidence;
  in your hands I seek refuge.
Protect my body and spirit,
  and show me your love always.
Eternal Father,
  your goodness is without limit or measure.
I rejoice to dwell safely in your heart.
My salvation consists in invoking you,
  and my happiness is your glory.
Accept my lifelong gratitude,
  Glorious and Eternal Father.
I praise you
  with all my being
  as your faithful child.
Amen.

Prayer on Contemplating Nature

You, O God, Majestic Creator,
    are the origin of all life.
Nothing can exclude itself
    from your creative influence.
You are wonderful in your words
    and in your sovereignty.
Amazed,
    I contemplate the perfection of the world
    you created for human beings.
You are unmatched in your power
    and in your goodness.
O Lord, you direct like a conductor
    the orchestration of a storm,
    and you shape like a sculptor
    the petals of a flower.
You are prodigious in your majesty
    and in your wisdom.
Lord, you have fashioned human beings
    to accept the challenges of nature
    and to be your voice in creation.
O Lord and King, Majestic Creator,
    you have made your mystery transparent
    in the world you have created.
I worship you
    in your creation
    and in your providence.
Amen.

Prayer in the Divine Presence

You, the Eternal One, are our God.
How insignificant we are in your presence.
Blessed are you, Lord,
Creator of the Universe,
who has finely fashioned nature
and with love made humankind
in your image.
Your deeds are eloquent and without equal;
your teachings our guide.
You have engraved your words in our hearts
and have pointed the paths to be followed.
Lord, teach us, your sons and daughters,
to love, respect, and live in union with this world.
Help to fill all our moments with useful deeds
in order to live
according to your laws.
Grant us, Almighty Lord, the desire
and the ability to hand on
your teachings to our children,
so that they, from generation to generation,
may praise your holiness and your grandeur.
Let us grow in wisdom, justice, and goodness.
Transform us into messengers of love
and builders of peace and harmony
in this world.
Amen.

Prayer at a Silent Moment

Lord, my God,
    in this special moment of complete quiet
    I open my soul to you.
I am grateful and happy
    for the benefit this moment of silence affords me.
Lord, my God,
    I did not always appreciate
    the grace of your serene presence.
Needlessly I gave myself up
    to the bombast and heated agitation
    that took me far from my deepest self
    and from you.
I withdraw now into the warm fold of your silence
    to better capture
    the gentleness of your presence
    and the rushing energy of your love.
Your silence fills up my being,
    makes me whole again,
    and redefines the ultimate meaning of my being.
Lord, you are eloquent
    in silence and soft whispers;
    strengthen me always with your silence
    so that I may build in peace
    all of my days.
Amen.

Prayer for Full Life

My encounter with you in prayer, Heavenly Lord,
   is not achieved in words,
   in the mere repetition of formulas
   learned by rote.
You are the Divine Interlocutor,
   worthy of my wholehearted attention
   and of the total openness of my being.
Lord, I relate to your loving presence
   in order to express all the feelings
   I carry with me.
You deserve my heart's best,
   my total sincerity and confidence,
   as I utter this prayer of a child.
Lord, may I focus on you totally
   so that I may absorb and live to the full
   this silent experience of my dialogue with you.
You know me and you love me infinitely;
   in you I find
   the supreme reason for my life.
Amen.

Prayer for Faith in Time of Doubt

I don't even know what to say, Blessed Lord,
    I am so confused.
I am caught in the midst of a violent crisis of faith,
    so uncertain and doubtful.
I am going through a difficult time
    in what touches the depth of my belief.
I am almost tempted to give in
    to impatience and despair.
Something within me cries out for you,
    yet you seem not to be there.
I have broken away from many childhood beliefs.
I decided to let my faith pass through the filter
    of my personal experience.
Suddenly, I found myself too far from you,
    from security and certainty.
If I still turn to you, Blessed Lord,
    it is because I have not yet lost
    the hope of finding
    an exit door
    for my spiritual anguish.
I begin to realize
    that by myself I will not be able to overcome
    life's ambiguities and contradictions.
I know the mystery of you continues,
    and that my faith-existence is a challenge
    to be embraced.

The light of your occasional shadowy presence
    makes me see that my crisis comes
    from the depth of my maturity,
    from the depth of my faith.
The irony, Lord:
    there is a crisis of doubt
    only because there is faith.
Perhaps I have become too demanding
    and too positive.
Open my heart now, Lord,
    to the right attitude
    when confronted with questions
    of my faith.
Amen.

Prayer for Perseverance

Help me, Faithful God, to conquer my inconsistency
   and to persevere in my duties.
Because of it I suffer
   and bring suffering to others.
Shore up my lack of will and tenacity.
You certainly know, my God,
   how complex my life is, any person's.
But this does not exempt me
   from the effort to carry out my obligations
   till they are completed.
Let me not stop half way, my God,
   because of laziness or cowardice.
Not all obstacles are insurmountable.
The ghost of failure should not scare me.
Let me not be prey to inertia, my God,
   when faced with obstacles
   that block the road to the goals I am to reach.
My will to persevere is always tested
   when I decide to carry out my plans.
Hold out, my Faithful God, your powerful hand
   if I weaken and want to give up.
Give me inner strength, my God.
On the road of perseverance,
   I am no hero.
Only allow me to taste the joy
   of ending successfully all my initiatives
   and activities.
Amen.

Prayer to God Within

Blessed are you, Lord, my God,
   who are not merely beside me
   but within me.
Nothing in the world compares to this reality.
It is part of your unique mystery,
   your unique intimacy.
Lord, my God,
   you hide the infinity of your eternal being
   in the small dimensions of my living createdness.
In the heart of my life
   you throb unceasingly with your creative power.
You are in everything I ponder, feel, and am.
There is no obstacle to your presence.
Lord, my God,
   you are the all that sustains me as I am.
You live within me
   and yet you do not obstruct
   my personal achievements.
Neither do you substitute for me
   and obliterate my identity.
Lord, my God,
   in the very depth of myself
   I belong to you;
   with you I write my history.
Amen.

Prayer to Recognize the Signs of God

Lord, I want to decipher your presence
    through the events and objects that make up my life,
    to express the impact
    that they have on me.
In this I am an interpreter of your creation.
I make use of images, signs, and comparisons,
    and I try to interpret your revelation
    in the daily events that surround me.
All along I am faced, Lord,
    with the mysterious signs of your passing by.
Permit me to see your footprints in my life,
    and to experience the joy of your presence.
Lord, events and objects sometimes pose questions
    and I have no answers.
Grant me some of your infinite capacity
    of seeing and proclaiming
    the truth and beauty
    of the beings you have created.
I want to absorb their message, Lord,
    in order to return them transformed
    into a conscious gift to your love,
    and thus proclaim your praise.
Amen.

Prayer for Uprightness

Lord, how I feel the need of your grace
    to preserve my uprightness.
Nothing is more valuable in life
    than this quality.
Even in the most common things
    I ought to mirror this inner quality.
It is this trait that gives me the chance
    to keep my life and everything in it
    clear and pure,
    maintaining it in its original state.
Lord, with this centralizing singlemindedness
    I may live in total harmony with you.
May everything in my life reflect this fundamental attitude.
Lord, I have often chosen
    the twisting roads of malice and criticism,
    of biased judgment and venomous interpretation.
Forgive me for having called
    so many brothers and sisters
    to stand up as defendants in my court,
    judging them,
    when I was the guilty one.
Restore, Lord,
    your complete dominion over my spirit.
Keep my ways of dealing with others highminded
    and full of respect.
Be a constant source of inspiration to my vision,
    my judgments, and my actions.
Help me to travel through life
    along the straight path
    of your justice and love.
Amen.

Prayer for Spiritual Concentration

God, I have strayed too far from myself,
    spreading myself thin on unworthy causes.
In order to return to the center of my being,
    I need to discipline myself.
Now I place myself in your presence;
    I want to focus my attention inward
    and come home to myself.
You, my God, afford me with the best way
    to find myself
    through the dialogue of prayer.
I want to develop the habit
    of stopping,
    being alone with myself,
    and taking a contemplative attitude
    that will draw me to my inner self.
Too often it looks as if I am not achieving anything,
    as if I am drifting without a rudder
    on life's seas.
I am sure, though, of my need
    not to live on the surface of myself.
Lord, I will dedicate myself
    to achieve this concentration.
Only in this way will I overcome
    my constant restlessness.
Grant me the grace of having access
    to my inner reality,
    and in this way reach calm and serene contact
    with you.
Amen.

Prayer for Spiritual Guidance

I want to praise you
in all I say and do, Lord and Creator.
Rest in me
so that my life
may be guided by your wisdom.
Direct my words
so that they may be just and clear
and not become soiled
by slander or lies.
Pierce my thoughts with the light
of your truth.
Sensitize my ears
so that I might hear the calls of the poor,
whose lives are plunged in need and fear.
Make me more understanding
of their limitations and desires.
Divine Counsellor, I pray you,
echo in the deepest recesses of my being
your friendly call,
indicating the right path to take
in the decisive moments of my life.
Only you can guide me aright.
Instill in me the thoughts and language of love,
which can be translated into concrete acts—
not remaining sterile "nice" words—
when I am faced with the higher demands
of human solidarity.
Amen.

Prayer to Love in Deed

Loving Lord, in your power which knows no limitations,
   grant me the happiness to love
   and to be loved.
If love starts with an eternal hope,
   lead me, then, to this hope.
Even if love is no more than a ghost,
   let me, then, have such marvelous visions of the heart.
Love is like a light:
   whoever does not see it, denies it.
Let me see and feel this light of love,
   in order to understand it.
Let my love
   be love that is visible.
Allow me, Lord,
   to love in spirit, in truth, in deed.
Light this fire of love in my soul and heart,
   revealing it in my speech,
   my eyes, my entire being,
   and in my silence.
Lord, you created the world with love;
   open the doors that lead to this love.
Amen.

Prayer of Praise
for the Gift of Life

I praise you, Lord,
   for the gift of life,
   which is renewed at every moment
   in all its beauty.
I love the life you gave me,
   with all that it stands for.
Lord, I feel in the depth of my being
   the unmatched joy of living.
Take some of my joy
   and distribute it among those
   who are sad and oppressed,
   who cannot enjoy their daily bread.
Even when someone close to me is cruelly snatched away
   in death,
   even then I want to bless you,
   because I believe that life always has the last word.
The power of life throbs in my veins,
   which you in your creative power
   mysteriously sustain day and night.
The gift of life is so great
   that it is beyond anything one might desire.
The greatest blessing, Lord, is to know how to say
   thank you for the gift of my life,
   letting me experience
   the deep joy of living.
Amen.

Prayer for a Mother

I thank you, Lord God,
    for the marvelous wealth of my mother's love.
She is alive always within my heart.
In a way, I still consider myself a babe,
    fit safe and cozy in her arms.
You gave me, Lord, this treasure
    which increased in value all through my life.
When I wake up,
    my thoughts instinctively fly to her,
    and I claim for her,
    Sovereign and Worshipped God,
    your most precious reward.
I am fully convinced that you, Lord,
    in offering me my mother's love
    gave me a glimpse of your infinite love.
I keep this maternal image forever in my heart.
My Lord, look after her,
    and fill the measure of happiness she deserves.
Enrich her with the bounty
    that only you can bestow.
Lord, my mother is your daughter;
    receive her into your arms;
    keep her forever in your heart.
Bless her forever,
    always devoted to you.
Amen.

Prayer for a Father

Blessed are you, O Divine Father,
    for giving me the one
    who shared with you in the creation of new life.
I thank you for the honor, the joy, and the happiness
    of having a good father,
    whose name is engraved in my heart.
Part of his being, I continue in life
    the traits of his character.
Favor me, O Heavenly Father, with the grace
    of letting me be faithful to this image
    which I carry within me.
The individual differences,
    which became more accentuated
    with the passing of time,
    will never detract from the heritage
    which I received from my father.
I want to keep, with affection and gratitude,
    the indestructible tie of my lineage.
Forgive me, O Heavenly Father, the faults I committed
    against my father.
Forgive me, if I did not live up
    to his hopes and efforts.
Forgive me, if sometimes I hurt his feelings
    and worried him.
You know, O Father, that I love him,
    that he is always in my heart.
Reserve for him a special blessing
    for all that he did
    and all that he will always be for me.
Amen.

Prayer for One's Children

My God, source of all life,
    thank you for the blessing you gave me
    when you entrusted me with children.
I have tried faithfully
    to live up to your expectations.
It is not for me
    but for each of them
    that I pray.
Care for them in your great kindness.
Wherever I am lacking,
    supply the blessing of your protection.
You see the sincere love of my caring,
    small as it is,
    compared with what they need and deserve.
In the name of this love,
    keep them, along the path of life,
    free from evil,
    and make them always strong, happy, and loving.
All of them, without distinction,
    are a living part of my being.
My God, I want them to be better than I am.
In the midst of the rich opportunities of life,
    may they count on your powerful help.
Every day, as I pray for my needs, my God,
    I am actually praying for them.
In total confidence I place them
    under your divine parental care.
Amen.

A Husband's Prayer

Blessed are you, my Gracious God,
    who gave me my wife;
    she became flesh of my flesh,
    blood of my blood.
I thank you for everything she stands for
    in my life.
Help me to understand, Lord,
    that because she is different from me
    and because of her unique qualities,
    she adds so much to what I am.
Her sensitivity and her love
    fulfill me harmoniously.
I promise, Lord, to stand next to her
    through life and to be a loving husband.
I thank you, Lord,
    for the way I am enriched
    by being in touch with her feelings.
I feel fulfilled and happy, Lord,
    when I can count on her warm presence,
    sharing in all the varied aspects of my life.
She has become part of my being.
I ask you, Lord,
    passionately protect our love for each other.
May it always remain
    faithful and strong.
Amen.

A Wife's Prayer

My God, I thank you for the husband
    you gave me.
I feel as if we were born for each other.
The happiness I feel
    also comes with the obligation
    to love him as he loves me.
With tenderness I keep the memory
    of our early encounters.
I recall our efforts to fit together
    and to understand each other.
Sometimes it seems to me, my God,
    that he is like the plant root
    and I am the plant.
He is never separated from my being
    and with time he more and more sustains my life
    and enriches it.
My God, take good care of him
    because I love him so much;
    I love him just as he is.
Faithful to him, I want to be worthy of his love
    and fulfill our common destiny
    to the very end.
I hope that with your grace, my God,
    I will live happily with him,
    side by side,
    fulfilling my role with all my heart.
Pour your blessing, my God,
    over my husband's life,
    over his work and concerns,
    and make our lives become even more beautifully united.
Amen.

cA Pregnant Woman's Prayer

Blessed are you, Lord, Creator of the Universe;
  you give life to human beings.
You created humankind in your image and likeness;
  you breathed in their nostrils
  love for all that lives.
Blessed are you, Lord, Merciful Father;
  you keep within my body
  the wonder of the human seed.
Thus you give life and form
  to my child.
Blessed are you, Lord, holy and kind;
  you allow me to reach the moment of childbirth
  with a steadfast and happy heart.
May the time stipulated by you
  for giving birth
  be an hour of health, peace, and tranquillity.
Blessed are you, Lord, our King and Savior;
  may the tears of concern and excitement
  bring forth your full blessing for my newborn.
Both of us, mother and baby, remain in your hands.
Blessed are you, Lord, Great and Sovereign God;
  give me the joy to care for my child.
May we live in happiness
  under your constant shining light
  and infinite love.
Amen.

Prayer for the Sake
of Children

I offer you, O God, the happiness of children,
  who innocently grow in the light of your eyes.
They are rightfully your favorites;
  for them you have an unlimited tenderness.
You care for each of them
  more than we can imagine.
My attitude toward them, too, influences
  their development.
Help me not to hamper with my impositions
  the free growth of the children's world.
Ease the task of parents and educators, I pray you.
Grant ample space for the creative spontaneity
  of these budding souls,
    so that they may grow in a world of freedom,
    understanding, and love.
Embrace them with the tenderness
  of your parental heart.
Help me conquer my impatience and selfishness,
  so that I may always have a gentle smile
  for all children that approach me.
For the sake of children, God,
  save this world from catastrophies and wars;
  and grant all human beings better days
  with peace and unity among all.
Amen.

A Youngster's Prayer

I need you, Lord, to carry out
    the plans and projects
    that are stored in my heart.
Counsel me as you well know how,
    because I don't want to fail or go wrong.
I need you, Lord, to help me choose
    the best road.
May others, too, respect my efforts
    and my wish to succeed.
I need you, Lord, to find
    the support and company of a loyal friend.
Preserve in me high spirits and easy
    communication with everyone,
    and save me from dangerous by-ways.
I need you, Lord, to conquer
    all the difficulties of my journey.
Bless my paths with your presence
    so that I may spread
    the strength of your love,
    wherever I am.
Amen.

Prayer for the Elderly

To you, my Great and Loving God, I lift this prayer
    for all those who are bent under
    the weight of years.
Your benign providence allowed
    their days on earth to be lengthened.
My God, now they look back
    and see the trodden path
    from their pranks as children
    to old-age pains.
Cancel all bitterness from their spirits
    so that they may recall
    the pleasant and happy memories.
Extinguish, my God, all signs of resentment
    caused by the malice or ingratitude
    of those who crossed their paths.
Bring joy to weary and depressed hearts.
Provide them with the means
    to revive the joys
    of normal and gregarious living.
My God, dispel those ghosts of solitude,
    forsakenness, and despair.
Surround them in their daily lives
    with human warmth
    and supportive help.
Let them keep an open and joyful disposition.
Reward, my God, the steady dedication of their lives
    with the blessing of that peace
    that can come only from you,
    a peace that prevails against all limitations
    of old age.
Amen.

A Sick Person's Prayer

I am ill, Lord;
   come and heal me.
You can protect me and free me
   from all those evils of body and mind.
I have confidence in your miraculous power;
   I invoke your name
   so that you can assist me
   in my distress
   and speed my cure.
Believe me, Lord,
   I am learning
   the great lessons of humaneness and patience,
   of gratitude and solidarity,
   which suffering brought me.
You, who are the source of all kindness
   and of all life,
   alleviate my pain.
Take away from me all shadow of depression,
   and strengthen my spirit,
   so that I can withstand everything
   without a word of despair or rebellion.
I am in your hands today as always.
Restore me, so that I may return
   to my work,
   to surroundings of family and friends.
I need healing, Lord;
   come and heal me.
Amen.

A Teacher's Prayer

God, our Master,
  you are the Supreme Teacher
  who illumines human beings with truth.
Blessed be your word of love.
God, our Father,
  make me your echo,
  and allow me to sow truth and goodness.
Blessed be your attitude,
  so full of understanding.
God, our Master,
  let me be passionate about beauty
  and truth,
  and warm my heart with your commandments.
Blessed be your light of truth,
  filled with blessings for us.
Grant me the gift of conveying,
  teaching, correcting, and indicating your ways,
  your shining, glorious kindness.
God, our Master,
  direct my mind to your truth,
  my hands to kind acts.
I am small and frail in your light,
  but allow me to fulfill my difficult mission.
Blessed be your mercy,
  which teaches us so much.
Amen.

A Physician's Prayer

Help me, Lord, to receive with respect,
　　understanding, and love,
　　all those who seek me
　　and are in need of assistance.
Help me, to accept life's mysteries
　　and to find answers to my doubts in your light.
Help me, Lord, to understand the agony
　　of those who are sick,
　　and to confront wisely
　　the problems of those who come to me.
May your inspiration always guide me.
Help me, to remain serene,
　　to be patient and clear-minded,
　　finding creative powers and faith
　　in your kindness.
Help me, in the midst of darkness and despair,
　　to uncover solutions
　　and to heal those who are ill.
May your help never fail me.
Help me, Lord, to respect and honor my oath.
Grant me unselfishness
　　and humility to serve.
Help me, always to be your
　　servant and messenger,
　　and thus alleviate human suffering.
May your kindness always accompany me.
Amen.

An Executive's Prayer

God, help me in my decisions
   and in the fulfillment
   of my tasks.
I want to be more humane and more sensible,
   keeping your kindness ever in mind.
God, help me to keep away
   from everything that is petty,
   alien and cruel,
   and to act according to your guidance.
Help me to be creative
   and to know how to make good use of teamwork.
May my work be always subject to your forgiveness,
   and under your blessed light.
God, forgive me my past errors.
   and guide me in the future.
Listen to my supplication
   and hear me in your mercy.
God, accept the words of my mouth
   and the thoughts and desires of my heart.
Bless me with success
   and direct me
   toward lasting goodness.
Amen.

A Worker's Prayer

Accept, Lord of the Universe, the prayer I raise to you
  in the name of all workers of the world
  who need your ongoing protection
  in the fulfillment of their tiresome tasks.
Lord, you desire the happiness of all your children;
  you want them to find fulfillment
  through the execution of some work.
May this work become ever more humane and dignified;
  may it provide security and well being.
May the workers accomplish their duties
  and may they see their legitimate wishes protected.
Every morning give them
  the renewed courage and energy
  to face each working day.
Bless their families, Lord of the Universe,
  and grant every worker joy and pleasure,
  so that they can dedicate themselves to their occupation
  without becoming prey
  to pessimism and discouragement.
Preserve their health and good spirits;
  strengthen the spirit of solidarity among them.
May their joint efforts be directed
  toward righteous and healthy aims,
  so that they might become a united family
  under your watchful eyes.
Amen.

A Driver's Prayer

Lord, Creator of the Universe,
 you, who determine and guide the destiny
 of human beings,
 give me your care and attention
 while I am driving.
You kindly accompany our journeys;
 give me quick and appropriate reflexes,
 when I speed or brake.
You illumine our routes with your love;
 give me always clear vision,
 when I need to see
 and avoid dangers.
Lord, Creator of the Universe,
 you are a true shield and support;
 give me patience, kindness, and understanding,
 when I am on the road.
Help me to realize
 that your presence and love is not only with me,
 but with those in the other vehicles also.
Amen.

Prayer for Courage

Lord, my maker, I am no superperson
  to endure everything without complaining.
You know that my strength is limited
  and lasts only so long.
Believe me, Lord, this is no excuse
  to avoid facing reality.
What I ask for, above all, is the courage to fight.
Lord, do not permit me to be a coward
  when facing day-to-day difficulties,
  or let me waver when confronting my duties.
Keep me from dramatizing difficult situations
  so that I may accomplish my tasks
  with serenity and peace.
Strengthen my determination
  to carry out my projects and responsibilities.
May my past trials become a positive balance
  of enriching experiences.
I trust in your help, Lord,
  that I may never fall prey to fear
  when facing these haunting dangers.
Gird me with your strength in the midst of my struggle.
Grant me the ability to keep up the good fight
  joyfully,
  without ever losing faith.
Amen.

Prayer for Faith

I ask you, my Blessed Lord, for yet another gift.
It's not something I can see in a store window,
    something that money can buy.
Kindle in me your divine light,
    a holy spark;
    I do not want to be like dust
    blown by the wind,
    or a stone that falls uncontrolled
    down a well.
I pray for the gift of faith.
Without faith, Blessed Lord,
    there is no work, no progress,
    no harmony or peace;
    we do not see the sunshine
    or the twinkling stars as we should.
But with faith
    I acquire the strength and the gift
    of making small things great,
    of taking casual events seriously,
    of distinguishing what is common and passing
    from what is everlasting.
The faith I need and pray for
    is the link between the sacred and the profane,
    the communion between you and humanity;
    it is the source of the love I want to sow.
Give me faith, Blessed Lord,
    so that it be part
    of my innermost being and infuse my heart and mind.
With faith I want to relish the sweetness of living,
    and taste holiness and joy.

This is the faith I long for and need,
    not as an escape from life,
    but as an inspiration and guide for life.
Lord, give me faith today and always;
    may it be to me a flame that burns
    all of my days.
Amen.

Prayer for Protection

Shield me, my Father and Mother;
    I am your child.
I turn to you with anxiety, seeking your protection.
Have pity and free me from this menace,
    so that my life does not become unbearable.
Do not allow my name
    and the names of those dear to me
    to be thrown into the gutter
    of calumny and meanness;
    take up my cause with your untiring love.
Soothe the furor of my anger
    when I am a victim of injustice
    and ingratitude.
Spare me from the humiliation
    of having to prove my innocence publicly.
Keep me from imitating the attitude
    of those who promote themselves
    at the price of other people's lives or reputations.
Let not the virus of jealousy and malice
    penetrate my intentions,
    corrupting them to the core.
Be my support and my defense, my Father and Mother.
Look after me on the road of life,
    and do not permit me to fall by the wayside,
    but guarantee me, today and always,
    your protection.
Amen.

Prayer of Thanksgiving

Thank you, Lord of the Universe,
    for all the gifts
    you always offer me.
Thank you for all I receive:
    for the water that washes me,
    for the clothes I wear,
    for the bread that sustains me.
For my dwelling and my parents,
    for my sisters and brothers,
    and for my friends.
For the knowledge gained from striving,
    and for the toils of each day.
For the good mornings that have dawned upon me,
    for the light that shines upon me,
    and for the handshakes that link me to others.
For the time you have allotted me,
    for the life you have offered me,
    and for the blessings of each new day.
Thank you for being with me, Lord,
    for listening to me,
    and for taking me seriously.
Thank you even for receiving today's thank you.
Thank you, Lord, thank you very much.
Amen.

Prayer for Divine Grace

God, our Father,
    the world is full of your glory;
    listen with pity to your child,
    who prays for your presence and protection.
God, our Father,
    wherever I turn
    I see your wonders;
    look at me, your child,
    who prays for your love and kindness.
God, our Father,
    all of nature sends out divine echoes;
    listen to the words of your child,
    who prays for your mercy and light.
God, our Father,
    the world receives your wisdom so graciously bestowed;
    entend your blessing over your child,
    who asks for the privilege of your grace.
Amen.

Prayer for Patience

Eternal God,
    it is not easy to continue
    praying and waiting
    when time flees by so fast
    and nothing of what I ask for happens.
Do not become cross at me if I lack patience.
You know well, Eternal God,
    that there are innumerable aspects of this world
    that I do not understand,
    that I find absurd.
Help me to persevere
    and not to lose faith;
    help me to be patient with all that surrounds me—
    with time, with others, and with myself.
Eternal God, you know that I do not intend
    to impose on anyone.
At times, though, I am too hasty,
    too demanding.
Teach me, Eternal God, to be as patient
    with others and myself
    as you are with me.
Amen.

Prayer to Use Time Well

I want to return to you, O God, and put to good use
    all the time you have given me,
    with all its moments that belong to you.
It is the good use I intend
    that makes it possible to offer it to you.
O God, I am happy for having filled
    my time with useful, healthy, and productive activities.
Save me from wasting time
    with my empty, barren laziness.
My life's span belongs to you,
    but it is of such short duration—
    mornings, afternoons, and evenings,
    light hours and dark minutes,
    work and rest.
Nothing of what happens in the span of my life
    escapes your power.
Grant me, O God, the ability
    to draw out of my allotted time
    a service to your glory,
    thus contributing to the constructive march
    of history
    and the union of human beings.
Turn all my time into time of loving.
From everlasting, O God,
    you determined the exact length of my time.
Grant me now the grace to fill it
    with free and generous activity,
    scheduling everything with wisdom.
Enrich my present time
    with your eternal love.
Amen.

Prayer for Personal Achievement

Lord, I carry within me the basic wish
    to fulfill myself as a person.
This is a noble ideal
    that you want me to achieve
    during my lifetime.
I feel I should bring to fruition
    my being's potential.
Only in this way will I be able
    to express the native traits
    of my personality.
You encourage me, Lord, with your inspiration
    and decisive influence.
Thus I can truly dedicate myself to this effort,
    which integrates and fulfills me.
I want to begin by always accepting myself
    as I am.
Keep far from me those ideas
    that overstep my true capacity by far.
Direct me in this tangle of life
    to what is truly beneficial
    for my growth.
Give me always the ability to see,
    without disguises and utopias,
    the reality of myself and that of others.
Help me, Lord, to be myself,
    and may I be so in the light
    of your justice, truth, and love.
Amen.

Prayer for Happiness

We all search for happiness.
What road should I take to find it, God?
Immersed in life, I am sometimes blind,
    sometimes deaf.
I come to you, Lord, to find the road.
Is it true, Lord, that happiness blossoms
    from the thorns of struggle and achievements?
That it is a distant horizon
    and as soon as I come close to it, it disappears?
That it depends on our soul's serenity?
Does happiness lie
    in the search for happiness?
In this uncertainty, in this darkness,
    help me, Lord.
Allow me to find it nearby,
    perhaps within me!
Let me live harmoniously with myself
    and with others.
God, give me the strength and the great joy
    of discovering the great secret of life:
    to do what is good,
    to serve others with joy,
    to sow love,
    and thus be able to realize
    that to live in this way is true happiness.
Amen.

Prayer Before
an Important Decision

Lord, Almighty God,
　　source of light, truth, and eternal goodness,
　　transform this present moment
　　into an hour of vision and inspiration.
Help me to find wisdom;
　　shed light on my thoughts.
May my aspirations come true
　　through righteous and good deeds.
Give me the strength to concentrate,
　　to think objectively,
　　and to see clearly.
Shed your light on me so that I may see
　　which decision to make.
Help me, O my Eternal God,
　　to avoid vanity and pride,
　　and thus be able to make worthy decisions
　　as a true child of yours.
Amen.

Prayer for a Sincere Life

I lift my thoughts to you, Lord my God,
    so that you may renew the sincerity
    of my way of life.
I want to restore, with your grace,
    the genuine image of my being,
    courageously, honestly acknowledging my value
    and my failings.
Lord God, I bring to your presence
    a burning wish to be a whole person
    without falsehood, deception, or duplicity.
Nurture in me an aversion to double dealing;
    diminish the gap that exists
    between my principles and my deeds,
    between my aspirations and my reality.
Heal me, Lord God, of the disastrous effects
    I cause by lack of thought or prudence.
Help me to carry my victories with simplicity
    and my defeats with courage.
Lord God, guard me from the blindness
    that comes from pride,
    for it closes my heart to understanding
    and acceptance of others.
Encourage me always to speak the truth,
    remain loyal to my convictions,
    and not give in to hypocrisy or dishonesty.
Bring me close to you, Lord God,
    and let me shine by the light of your Being,
    without shadow or blame.
Amen.

Prayer After Success

With an overflowing heart
    I thank you, the Source of all good,
    for the success I have achieved.
My spirit is filled with peace
    because you saw my hopes
    and answered my supplications.
My efforts were not in vain.
Kind Father, your grace helped me
    mysteriously,
    leading me to this successful conclusion.
What a pleasant task it is
    to express my deep gratitude
    for your sovereign wisdom and goodness.
I feel enriched by your visit.
You looked upon your child
    with infinite love;
    now my happiness is plain to see.
Kind Father, you taught me once again,
    through experience,
    that you never forsake
    those who place their trust and anxieties in your hands.
You do not overlook human frailty;
    without you I would not have been able
    to celebrate this achievement.
Accept the grateful heart of your child
    which overflows with gratitude
    and happiness.
Amen.

Prayer After Failure

O my God, in order not to cry my heart out,
  I want to direct my shout to you.
Help me to overcome the bitterness of failure.
I need to feel your presence
    close to me.
I cling to the hope that you
    will not cease to offer me opportunities,
    even when everything in my life seems to crumble.
I need to gain more experience.
Come with your grace
    to comfort and save me.
You, O my God, know well the heart
    that speaks to you,
    the good will of this child of yours.
If nothing turned out right,
    it was not for lack of effort.
My God, you know why this failure came about,
    and you do not want me to stand paralyzed
    and sad,
    as if standing amid the ruins of my life.
You want me to be strong, to continue with my life.
I ask you, O my God, grant me your help.
With you I will start anew,
    and will not stop on the way,
    turning my life into a wasteland.
If failure came,
    let me abide in the belief, O my God,
    that it was only to make me truly mature.
Thank you, my God.
Amen.

Prayer During Loneliness

Lord, I feel like a traveler in the desert,
    utterly alone.
I know that there are people close by,
    but it seems as if I live on an island
    without inhabitants.
You know that I cannot endure it any more;
    that is why I speak to you
    with all my heart's strength.
Already I feel, Lord—
    from the moment I uttered
    the first words to you—
    that I am coming out of my solitude.
How good it is to escape the trap
    of a sick and heavy solitude
    and meet with you.
Lord, you reassure me
    that I am never alone.
You are always with me,
    my sure companion
    in hours of insecurity.
Lord, you silence does not mean
    that you are distant.
Your invisible company never leaves my side.
I need only be more attentive
    to your presence.
Amen.

Prayer for Repentance

O God, full of mercy,
    you reign in the heavenly heights;
    I, your feeble creature—
    in low spirits, full of anxiety, despair, and darkness,
    on wandering tormented paths—
    have sinned.
I yielded to so many sins
    and have committed so many transgressions,
    openly and in secret.
How can I justify my sins?
What can I say in my defense?
In front of you, Lord, Supreme Judge,
    I stand as an accused,
    confessing all my weaknesses and care-less attitudes,
    prodded by passionate hate or perturbed emotion,
    by abuse of confidence,
    by lies and lack of love.
My God, how ashamed I am,
    and penitent.
Help me to stop my wrongdoing,
    and let my transgressions be blotted out
    by your great compassion.
You are a parent
    who forgives the sins of the children.
God, Lord of the living and of the dead,
    always be merciful;
    forgive me; absolve and purify me.
Give me strength and faith
    to find new directions in my life.
May they be illumined by your light, justice, and kindness.
Amen.

Prayer to Resist Violence

I ask you to grant me, O God of Peace,
  the necessary strength not to bend
  when faced with all the forms of violence
  in today's world.
When I feel directly attacked, Lord,
  do not allow despair to weaken my resolve,
  or fear to diminish my faith.
Gird me with your grace and fortitude,
  so that I can endure in the face of enmity,
  treason, and perverse blows.
Preserve, O God of Peace, in my spirit
  the firm will to fight
  with the arms of truth, justice, and love.
Renew my enthusiasm for good causes
  when faced with the menace of evil.
Place me among the forces
  of those whose battle for the coming of a new era:
  when hate and violence will not divide
  the human family any more;
  when understanding and fraternity
  will reign in the hearts of all.
Open my heart to the outcry of those
  who are persecuted and downtrodden.
Kindle in me, O God of Peace, the spark of high purpose,
  of constructive and noble ideals.
Help me to cooperate in the victory
  of a solid and harmonious peace program
  among all human beings.
Amen.

Prayer to Preserve Mental Balance

My God, there are complex and deep energies
  within me.
I come to beg you
    to help me channel these energies
    toward an integrated development of my being.
May these psychic energies work
    within the framework of a wholesome,
    balanced, and healthy process.
I am constantly exposed
    to the aggressive influences
    of people and circumstances.
I need, my God, great endurance
    in order not to become mentally ill.
I come to you, who are harmony itself,
    immutable and eternal,
    to help me reach the goal
    of a balanced, mature, and happy life.
Free me, my God, from the piling up of conflicts,
    which impede the harmonious expansion
    of my personality.
My God, I want to nurture thoughts and wishes
    that will ensure a clear orientation
    to my inner world.
Hear my plea so that I may serve you
    with all my heart;
    sustain me, my God, in my effort.
I will always count on your powerful help
    to further my well being
    and my human development.
Amen.

Prayer Before a Test

My God, enable me to trust in the good outcome
    of the test I am about to take;
    help me to contribute my own share
    of optimism and confidence.
With your grace, my God,
    I hope to crown my efforts with success.
Keep far from me at this moment
    any presumption that it all depends
    exclusively on me.
You are next to me, my God,
    the necessary and welcome presence
    in all the moments of life.
I will take this test, my God,
    because it is important
    for my personal development.
My God, be the source of my inspiration
    in my doubts and uncertainties,
    supporting me with your blessing.
Amen.

Prayer to Calm the Spirit

Calm me down, Lord, with your presence.
Open my heart to the smooth flowing
	of your serene spirit.
I am grateful to find this calm moment
	in your presence.
For I have been too excited,
	too busy with many activities.
I want to rest, Lord, in the shade
	of your power and love.
Restore my strength as only you know how.
Lord, I entered the battle with all my heart,
	and did not shrink from helping others
	who needed me.
Your kindness now rests on me
	like the pacifying blessing I have been yearning for.
No disquiet stirs in me,
	because you lead me to the sweet repose
	of a clear and quiet conscience.
I try to fulfill my part in creation
	and in the harmony of life.
Lord, overshadow me with your blessing.
Working side by side with my brothers and sisters
	for a better world,
	I find the meaning of my life.
Give me the opportunity to soothe my spirit.
I take refuge in you, Lord.
Amen.

Prayer to Discover the Meaning of Life

God All-powerful,
  let me perform the small tasks of my life
  in the spirit that can move mountains.
Reveal to me the secret
  of a happy and meaningful life,
  so that I will be at peace with nature
  and all people.
Free me from complaining about the past
  and worrying too much about the future,
  and grant me the blessing of understanding,
  so that I may live a happy present.
Grant me the opportunity to achieve
  a positive fulfillment of my tasks.
Open my ears so that I can listen to others;
  teach my heart to respect others
  and allow me to be respected in return.
Grant me good and sincere friends,
  with whom I can learn and share
  the hopes of life.
Allow me to love my neighbor, All-powerful God,
  and thus find the true meaning of life.
Amen.

Prayer for the Suffering

God, Compassionate Master,
   we yearn for a sign
   of your presence,
   for your compassionate voice,
   and your benevolent action.
Your mercy testifies to your love.
In your hands are our fates and lives.
Listen to our plea.
God, you always sustain the needy,
   and hear the plea of the forsaken;
   let there be comfort for those who suffer.
Give strength and faith to those who call unto you,
   endurance and patience to those who need it.
May your presence shine upon them always.
Without your help there is no comfort or cure,
   or medicine to alleviate pain,
   nor the means to relieve the weak and the suffering.
Hear this petition, O God of Compassion, and have mercy;
   alleviate the pain of those who suffer,
   so that they may rise and bless
   your infinite kindness.
Amen.

Prayer for the Poor

Almighty Father, I entrust to you the anguish
 of all the poor in the world.
Remind me of the great lesson
 that poverty teaches in human lives.
I need to acquire goods
 because I do not own anything;
 you, O Father, do not need anything
 because you have everything.
True wealth is in being what I am,
 even in the midst of shortage.
My dignity is not measured
 by the sum of my possessions;
 you want me as I am,
 without the trappings
 that result from buying and selling.
Teach me, your child, O Father, to love
 the true values of life.
I turn to you, full of confidence,
 in the name of those who suffer deprivation.
Save them through justice
 and through the generosity of those who are better
endowed.
Implant in us the realization
 that this life is not everlasting,
 that there is a pressing need
 to practice fairness and universal solidarity.
Almighty Father, awaken in our hearts
 the will to serve
 and deep compassion.
Look with special care
 on those brothers and sisters who are in need.
Amen.

Prayer for the Hungry

Lord, Mother Earth produces enough
   to satisfy the needs of every living being,
   but human ambition distorts your divine purpose.
Countless of your creatures go hungry every day.
Wealth and poverty, power and submissiveness
   coexist,
   but a lack of compassion, sensitivity, and love prevails.
Lord, you created the same laws for all human beings,
   but some do not heed your laws,
   but carry on blind and deaf to them.
The obsession to own
   and the ambition to own always more,
   and the fear of losing it
   create envy and anguish.
Lord, we humbly pray
   that your children may live in your light
   with your love,
   always in peace and freedom
   and without hunger.
Amen.

Prayer for the Sick

Compassionate Lord, I am deeply concerned
    with the health of someone dear to me.
My greatest wish
    is that this person may resume work
    and a normal life with family and friends.
Lord God, Merciful God,
    with insistence I commend this person's health
    to your care.
My prayer arises from the bottom of my heart
    to you, the source of life and salvation.
I know you do not rejoice
    in the affliction of your children.
My anxiety does not lead me to despair
    because I trust you.
Grant me what I confidently beg of you.
My heart will proclaim your praise.
I place in your hands, Lord God, Merciful God,
    the fate of this sick person,
    who has been suffering so much.
Speed the happy day of recovery.
Already now,
    touched by the knowledge of your compassion,
    I bless your holy name.
Amen.

Prayer for the Dying

God, Merciful Father,
  you always sustain us
  in our difficult and tragic hours.
Have mercy on your child who is dying.
Life is your gift,
  a loan to us who are mortal.
Your glance lightens our anguished hearts.
Have mercy on your child who is dying.
In your hands we entrust our spirit
  when we sleep and when we are awake.
You are our stronghold and our refuge.
Have mercy on your child who is dying,
  Merciful Father.
We are pilgrims traveling to eternity;
  while our final words are being spoken,
  have mercy on your child who is dying.
Amen.

Prayer for the Dead

All-powerful God—
    who has made human beings
    in your image and likeness,
    and has forever engraved our existence
    with your kindness—
    you give life and you take it back.
We are like a flower in the field:
    we blossom with the sun and water
    and we are gone with the wind,
    for human life is transient in this world.
You sow life in all the corners of the earth.
    and you call us unto your heavenly court.
We cry bitterly for our losses.
May the sacred memory of the deceased be our light.
May our silent invocation, our tears,
    our undying memory,
    together with the faithful image of our dear one,
    accompany us all our days.
O God, in your mercy answer us;
    make it possible for our brothers and sisters
    who are not with us any more
    to rest in the celestial peace.
May the memories of their lives stay with us;
    may they be a constant blessing
    and an undying heritage.
All-powerful God, Lord of Life and Death,
    turn our hearts toward those we love so much.
May their nostalgic and blessed memory
    become an incentive to our deeds,
    today and always.
Amen.

Prayer for Mourners

Lord, God of Life, you have called to your side
    a very dear and unforgettable person,
      whose passing away left a great emptiness in us.
There are those who are lost in sorrow.
I lift my prayer to you,
    God of Consolation,
      asking you to send comfort and help
    to the mourners.
Remind them that death is not the end of everything,
    and that at death a human being
      steps through to reach the peace
    of eternal life.
Lord God, restore serenity to the mourners' spirits;
    renew hope in the depth of their consciousness.
Inspire them with the thought of honoring
    the memory of the dear one
    who was called to your presence.
Sustain the faith in their hearts,
    so that they do not surrender to despair
    and to the sterility of angry complaints.
Lift high their will to live
    and to continue their daily tasks.
May they grow in valor.
Lord God,
    inspire us with the courage of the departed.
Make fruitful that person's way of living
    and dying
    now that it has been watered by the tears
    of pain and nostalgia.
Amen.

Prayer for Orphans

I offer you, our Mother and Father,
    the hidden and heavy suffering
    that burdens an orphan's heart.
I feel part of that unspeakable pain
    that makes them feel different
    and isolated in the world.
Ease the pain of their hearts
    through the friendship
    of unselfish people.
Comfort each one of them
    with your benevolence
    so that they may become
    neither downtrodden, perverted, nor neglected.
Come, our Mother and Father, with your benign help;
    surround them with the comfort
    and affection they need.
For those who need it most,
    reserve your choice blessing
    and most tender protection.
Amen.

Prayer for Catastrophe Victims

Have pity, Almighty and Merciful God,
   on all the poor victims of this disaster,
   which caused such unspeakable loss and pain.
Almighty and Merciful God,
   you are sensitive
   to human tears and pain,
   without reservation.
With your powerful assistance,
   come to everyone's rescue;
   deliver those who are injured,
   and soothe the victims of this tragedy.
Come to save those seriously affected;
   bring them indispensable medical aid.
Comfort the hearts of those who mourn,
   and, with your grace,
   Almighty and Merciful God,
   make this awesome trial bearable.
Amen.

Prayer for Refugees

God, you created human beings in your image,
    expecting them to find the path of life
    in the light of your presence;
    have pity on those without shelter or homeland,
    who live as refugees throughout the world.
God, you created human beings free;
    grant them the strength to withstand their trials.
Lead them from slavery to freedom,
    from darkness to light.
God, you created human beings with love;
    they are your children.
Protect those who are without a home;
    give them life, health, and peace,
    so that they might find their rightful road in life.
You created human beings
    to be brothers and sisters;
    grant hope and protection to those
    who are oppressed and suffer tribulation.
May they find loving hands to comfort them
    and a place to call home.
God, you create human beings
    and never abandon them;
    rescue them in their time of trouble.
Fill with your courage and faith
    all suffering refugees.
Amen.

Prayer for Prisoners

Make known, Lord God, your great mercy
    to those who are inmates in prison.
They are in great need of your help.
I want to visit them spiritually,
    through this prayer,
    inspired by humane and compassionate feelings.
Lord God, save those who accept their guilt;
    sustain with your strength
    those who rebel and run the risk
    of serious and radical perversion.
Grant that all those who are imprisoned
    may truly desire a better life,
    and rediscover the road to integrity.
Be for all of them, Lord God,
    the supreme comfort in their hour of despair
    and a profound source of hope.
May they discover in prison,
    with your grace and forgiveness,
    the strength of your merciful presence.
Amen.

Prayer for Victims
of Injustice

Creator of the Universe,
   you have bequeathed unto us
   your commandments, your laws,
   and your teachings of justice.
You entrusted human beings to be your messengers,
   protectors of the weak,
   and servants of just causes.
Your light illumines our minds,
   reminding us always
   that life is based on justice.
Allow us, Lord, today and always,
   to have our souls kindled with zeal for your law.
Allow us not to forget your covenant,
   and instead of sin,
   let us dedicate ourselves to purity and kindness.
Allow us, Lord, to become more alert to events
   that go against your laws of justice.
Allow us to become fully conscious
   of our responsibilities,
   and thus conquer calumny
   by confronting lies with honest action.
Allow us, Lord, to be humble and hope-filled
   when, with your wisdom,
   we defend the victims of injustice.
Grant us courage, strength, and prudence
   to be worthy messengers
   of your eternal justice and truth.
Amen.

Prayer to Work
for Goodness

Blessed are you, Lord,
    for employing human beings to reach others
    and to spread goodness.
You speak through their human words and deeds.
Show how much you love your children, Lord,
    by encouraging them
    to fulfull their tasks.
I sincerely accept my share of responsibility
    in this joint effort of your faithful ones,
    who labor so that goodness may prevail
    over evil.
I am aware, Blessed Lord,
    that you have a certain predilection
    for those who know you not.
Like weak and problematic children,
    they are the special aim of your parental care.
Entrust me, Blessed Lord, with this care
    through my loving initiatives
    and beneficial tasks.
I want to be part of the effort
    that will reveal you more,
    showing your love to all
    and reflecting your happiness.
Since you regard human collaboration,
    so highly,
    accept my wish, Blessed Lord,
    to spread goodness in the world.
Amen.

Prayer at Harvest Time

I believe in your blessing, Bountiful God,
    which you bestow upon those
    who toil in the fields,
    upon those who bring forth the produce
    which is indispensable to human life.
I hope for your protection, Lord God,
    which will assure us the best results,
    a rich harvest,
    compensating for all our efforts and sacrifices.
I trust in your grace, Lord God,
    which never fails to assist
    human productive endeavors.
We thus become your helper
    in the good use of nature's bounty.
I believe, hope, and trust, Lord God,
    that, thanks to you,
    we will have excellent harvests
    all over the world.
Amen.

Prayer to Humanize Life

You have helped me understand, Majestic Lord,
    that whenever human beings try to be human,
    they eventually find
    your divine face.
I dedicate myself to the task
    of making life on earth more human,
    and thus deserve the eternal bliss
    you promise.
I desire to participate, Lord,
    in the search for the true values
    that make it possible for us human beings
    to open a window to meet you.
I accept my share
    in the great humanizing task
    of establishing the link with your love.
Come, O Lord, with your help,
    so that our transient and imperfect living
    may be transformed
    by sharing in the enduring joy of your life.
Amen.

Prayer for the Spread of Truth

Although my field of action is restricted,
   O Lord, may I always exert some influence
   on the thoughts and deeds of others.
My God, make me a courier of your truth
   in every word and in every gesture,
   so that I may succed
   in raising in some small way
   the knowledge and understanding
   of those who surround me.
Inspire me with an abhorrence
   of all forms of falsehood and hypocrisy.
I wish to love those
   who may be in error or hypocritical;
   help me to inspire them
   to love honesty and to seek truth.
I accept, my God, the responsibility
   to take part in deeds of justice and love.
Since these are the fruits of your truth,
   they dignify and encourage us, your children.
My God, I am a servant of your truth;
   I desire to spread it as a life-giving message,
   bringing all people to noble aspirations
   and awakening in them
   a true community spirit.
Amen.

Prayer for the City

Protect, O Saving God,
    the city in which I live and toil,
    and all those who live in it.
Inspire, Lord,
    with constant dedication
    those who work for the city's welfare.
Forgive, Lord,
    those who are destroying it;
    keep us safe from their negative tendencies.
Protect us, in our homes and streets
    from burglaries, muggings, and killings.
Inspire us, Lord,
    to find solutions to protect our environment
    and to improve our human relations.
Show compassion,
    for the poor, the homeless, the neglected,
    and for the forsaken children.
Take care, O Saving God,
    of this seemingly faceless crowd,
    and grant order and peace to our city.
Amen.

Prayer for a Community

Blessed are you, God
    who have created us
    and given us life.
Blessed are you
    who have shed light on our visions and aspirations,
    and given us the means to find sustenance
    and to survive.
Blessed are you,
    who have given us marvelous ways to work
    and also the challenge and ability
    to overcome obstacles.
Blessed are you, God of the Universe;
    you guide and unite us,
    and make it possible for us to work together.
Be merciful with those you created;
    give us peace, harmony, and love in this life.
Be merciful and benevolent
    with all who need your guidance and love.
Be merciful in your infinite understanding,
    so that we may be united in our shared hopes.
Be merciful,
    so that all communities
    may live in hope in your light
    and under your infinite blessing.
Amen.

Prayer for the Progress of Science

Lord, Creator of all that is good,
    all the miracles we witness are your handicraft;
    they confirm your presence in the universe.
The sky, the clouds, the sun, the moon
    were all created by your goodness
    for the benefit of human beings.
How wonderful is the singing of the birds
    and the aroma of the flowers,
    a gift to humans for their delight.
Our bodies are magnificent machines,
    a sign of your work on our behalf.
Physicians discover cures
    and scientists beneficial new knowledge;
    it is all the unfolding process
    of your inspiration and guidance.
Roads become shorter, communications quicker,
    giving to people everywhere
    new and greater creative opportunities.
You, Lord, continually shine upon
    the work of researchers and philosophers,
    empowering them with light and inspiration.
I beg you, Lord, Great Creator and Innovator,
    show mercy and love for all your servants,
    our scientists.
Continue granting them your help
    so that the progress of science
    may be for the true benefit of humanity
    and a song of praise to your infinite wisdom.
Amen.

Prayer for the Development of Culture

Lord God, human thought searches
 to understand more and more
 of the meaning of life
 and the destiny of the world.
Help us in our constant endeavor
 with the light of your truth and spirit.
Lord, for our individual and social living,
 we strive to develop
 sound principles and norms of conduct.
Guide us in these pursuits
 with the infallible security of your divine vision.
Lord God, the progress of human culture
 accompanies the march of history;
 it obeys the universal yearnings
 of community, justice, and peace.
Open it up to the progress of love,
 fueled by the power of your grace.
Amen.

Prayer for International Harmony

God of Peace, how difficult it must be
    to reign over the world,
    which is so disunited
    and composed of so many heartless people.
How sad it must be to see so many
    misguided, abandoned, and hungry people.
How pitiful to find so many walls
    erected around people,
    to see so much war-born blood and misery.
How unpleasant it must be
    to hear so many
    lamentations and anguished cries.
Allow me, Lord, to help in the great task
    of opening new roads
    and shedding some light on dark corners
    of the world.
Allow me to be united
    to the tired and separated,
    to sow a little love among all people.
Allow me, Lord, to be your servant and partner
    in this mission;
    fill me with strength and courage
    to fulfill some small part
    of what you desire
    and I long for.
Allow me to be a bridge-builder
    in this great task of encouraging
    harmony among nations.
Amen.

Prayer for Our Country

Bless, O Father, our God and Lord,
    all your children
    who live in this country.
May the ties of fellowship be strengthened,
    making us one family.
Free us, O Father,
    from fatal catastrophies and disasters.
Unite us in peaceful struggle
    toward true progress and prosperity;
    may it become reality
    through the productive work of all.
Shine your light, O Father,
    upon all those responsible
    for the destiny of this nation.
Spread your spirit of peace
    over the length and breadth of this great land.
Preserve, O Father,
    the welcoming spirit and hospitality
    that characterizes the tradition of our people.
Help us to preserve the climate of freedom,
    justice, and opportunity for all.
Protect, O Father, our God and Lord,
    all citizens;
    encourage them in their efforts
    in the cities and rural areas,
    along our borders and on the world scene,
    and thus build a happy and beneficial future
    for all our citizens.
Amen.

Prayer for Security

In the giant conglomerate,
  the cold jungle of glass skyscrapers,
  in the ocean of electronic devices,
  do not abandon, Lord, the human being,
  so isolated on this sunless island.
Grant, All-powerful God, that in the frenzy
  of a mad and inhuman daily race
  of pressures, agitation, and polemics,
  the human being might find time
  to think about you, the Creator.
Let malice be turned into kindness;
  let rulers begin hearing and understanding
  their human subjects.
Let the violent find tranquillity and clear vision.
Let all regain the security of the home.
Let robberies and muggings cease,
  and let dialogue and good will take their place.
Let children and adults regain their happiness,
  and find consolation, peace, and love.
Grant, O God, that forests and flowers may grow again
  and the cleansed river waters continue
  to breed their fish;
  may the sun and the skies
  not be covered by the cloud of pollution,
  and may we breathe again without fear.
In our land,
  so badly shattered by ruthless competition,
  make a miracle come true:
  bring about a deep transformation
  and grant, O God, your blessing and your light.
Amen.

Prayer for Rulers

Father of the Universe, you created the cosmic order
and human creatures to be your co-workers.
You, who gave human beings their intelligence
and creativity,
offer your light to those who lead and govern.
You know how hard their task is
to be always watchful, just, and humane,
moderate, flexible, and compassionate.
They need your guidance and your help.
Grant them, O God, your love
and your benevolence;
make them sensitive and attuned to your will.
May they become instruments of justice and freedom,
and true sowers of goodness in ther work.
Kindle in them the will to serve;
fortify their capacity for self-sacrifice.
Teach them to defend just causes
through correct and faithful behavior.
Lord God, you are the guardian of liberties
and teacher of grand ideals and fellowship;
bless them and protect them;
sustain them with the light and perfect peace
that emanate from heaven.
Amen.

Prayer for Religious Leaders

Lord, our God, I ask for the grace
  of your light
  for the leaders of all religious confessions.
Illuminate them in the fulfillment
  of their sacred tasks.
May their hearts be filled with great love.
Lord, our God, I plead for your special protection;
  guard them in the exercise of their ministry.
Through this prayer, Lord, our God,
I share, with all of them, the weight of responsibility
  that lies on their shoulders.
Strengthen them with your power and wisdom.
I especially recommend to you
  those whose duty is burdened by difficult situations.
Show them the right path,
  and sustain their energy.
Lord, our God, I invoke for them your blessing
  that they may become true enablers
  of human community.
Sustain them in their faith
  and grant them your reward.
Amen.

Prayer for Peace

Blessed are you, King of the Universe,
 who has created this world.
Generation after generation,
 human beings praise your deeds.
Your powerful actions proclaim love to all.
Through the words of prophets and psalmists,
 you have announced to all the world
 the value, importance, and the need for peace.
Show and teach us, Lord, your paths
 that lead all peoples
 to understand the value of peace.
You listen with love
 and protect the weak and downtrodden;
 you teach the value
 of freedom, justice, and fellowship.
We witness your endless dedication to humanity
 and your eternal love.
We proclaim your glory and we sing your praises,
 aware of your kindness and the miracles you perform.
We beg you, Lord our God,
 for the miracle of true peace.
Light our way so that we may find it.
Grant us this peace,
 which is your most precious gift.
Plant virtue in all our souls
 and turn us into pioneers of true peace.
Amen.

Prayer of Those Seeking God

Creator of the Universe,
   the world seems to step toward chaos.
People give the impression that, more and more,
   they are losing their common sense and balance.
Humankind needs your help.
Have mercy on us,
   and accept our heartfelt words,
   for we truly seek you, Lord, our God.
Do not reject us from your presence.
Do not withdraw your holy spirit from us,
   or your infinite kindness.
For we truly seek you, Lord, our God.
Give us a sign of your grace,
   and do not abandon us in difficult times
   or take away our strength.
For we seek you, Lord, our God.
Creator of the Universe,
   the world needs your guidance and grace.
Be our rescue, our comfort, our hope.
We seek you
   because we need your gracious assistance.
Amen.

Prayer for Unity

Father and Mother of all human beings,
    you are one and the parent of all.
There are more frequent signs
    that people are drawing closer to one another.
I am grateful for it.
Overcoming hostile divisions has become
    more frequent in our times.
I identify completely with this tendency.
Lord, I believe that the search for unity
    should be based, above all,
    on your will
    and should meet the higher demands
    of our calling to human solidarity.
I recognize the value of our different gifts
    that produce human and religious enrichment.
Help us to achieve the unity you desire.
Father and Mother of all human beings, One God,
    make real our yearning for the unity of people
    everywhere.
Amen.

Prayer of Thanks for Friends

I want to thank you, Gracious Lord,
　　for the good friends you give me;
　　they are for me a priceless bounty.
Thanks to them, friendship is neither an abstraction,
　　nor a distant, almost impossible, dream.
I owe to your providence, Lord,
　　the possibility of counting on
　　the constant help of friends.
Between me and them you have formed a solid bridge,
　　which can withstand all threats of destruction.
The happiness with which you have blessed us
　　enables us to enrich one another.
Lord, there was something astonishing,
　　almost mysterious,
　　in the way I met my friends;
　　it was always outside the expected pattern.
But you alone know the reasons
　　that drew us closer together.
This surprise and joy are refreshing,
　　and I experience them anew
　　at every step of my life.
Not all proved to be steadfast friends,
　　but I have to thank you
　　for the faithful ones.
I promise to do everything in my power
　　to deserve this precious gift
　　that you have reserved for me.
I ask you, Gracious Lord, to keep them safe in your hands,
　　for they are yours above all.
Amen.

ͼPrayer for Sharing

Teach me, O Father,
  to work for the cause of the common person.
Correct me
  when I am tempted to make someone poorer
  so that I may prosper.
Open my eyes, O Father,
  to my brothers' and sisters' needs.
Remind me always of the common link among all people
  and of the law of universal solidarity.
Keep far from me the pettiness
  of selfishness.
Stretch to its limit my capacity
  to use my means in favor of common efforts.
Keep me alert, O Father, to the rights
  of the weaker people,
  the poor and powerless.
Lead me to the understanding
  that I should channel my energies
  to deeds of justice, mercy, and peace.
O Father, the gifts of the earth give witness
  that your love is directed to everyone.
Help me to share my material and spiritual treasures
  in order to translate into practice
  your commandment of love.
Open wide my heart's capacity for love and compassion.
Make me understand that I do not have
  a monopoly of your blessings,
  and that I should share with others
  the joys of life.
Amen.

Prayer for Fellowship

Creator of all human beings, Worshipped Lord,
  open the eyes and hearts of all your children
  so that they might see clearly
  and understand effectively
  the pressing need to live as brothers and sisters.
You are the one who insistently orders
  and encourages us to form on earth
  one human family.
Strengthen, Kind Creator, the precious ties of union.
You expect us to abhor all forms of fanaticism,
  and to cultivate the genuine spirit of our convictions.
O God of Infinite Love,
  help us in our efforts to realize
  our ideals of liberty, tolerance, and understanding.
You want us faithful to truth and human rights
  and far from disrespect and discrimination.
Beyond and above all differences,
  grant that we may stress
  the similarities that bring us closer.
After a dark past, you helped us discover
  our common spiritual heritage.
You helped us see the advantages of following
  the shining road of fellowship:
  the divine blessing and hopeful promise
  of a peaceful world.
Amen.

Prayer for Reverence for the Bible

O God, Eternal Teacher,
   in every situation of my life
   you shine upon me with the light
   of your eternal word.
The words preserved in the holy pages of the Bible
   mark the meeting point of all children
   with their celestial parent.
Let me proclaim the constant relevance
   of the holy book,
   always up to date
   in its inexhaustible spiritual fecundity,
   its extraordinary prophetic value,
   and the power of its divine message.
I praise you, Lord and Teacher,
   because you come to meet us on each venerable page.
Each page speaks of your love
   for human beings,
   and of your wisdom revealed in our history.
I find in the holy text of the Bible
   the pure and constant nourishment of my spiritual life.
I find in it the shining light
   that guides and comforts me
   on my terrestrial journey.
I revere your word, O God, Lord and Teacher,
   which is contained in the treasure of the Holy Bible.
I beg you to make the Bible always
   the place where, more and more,
   unity and fellowship converge.
Amen.

Prayer for Religious Dialogue

Being of all beings, Lord of all lords,
   you are the blessed and supreme light
   of all the peoples of the world.
I bless you and thank you
   for the new atmosphere of dialogue
   that you have encouraged among the world's
   religions and cultures.
Through our common defense of universal values,
   you fostered in us a sincere and conscious search
   for the things that unite us.
We now see that our motives are capable of uniting
   all people of good will and faith
   in a common effort toward peace.
Source of Life and Sun of Truth,
   you are the divine and eternal force for all hearts.
I praise you and exalt you
   for the clear understanding of the interdependence
   of human beings and nations.
Favor us with providential and effective means
   to overcome aggressive confrontation
   and the spirit of opposition.
Grant us the willingness to abandon
   polemic positions and obsessive fanaticisms,
   which destroy dignity, nobility, and human togetherness.
Infinite Grandeur and Eternal Goodness,
   you are the ultimate and decisive key of human history.
I thank you and glorify you
   for the hope you have instilled in us,
   for a world in which respect,
   liberty, and universal cooperation will reign.

Guide and help the work of religious leaders
 who try, with clear minds and generous hearts,
 to find a constructive and healthy path
 to sincere dialogue—
 the path of dialogue among people
 of all creeds, cultures, and traditions.
Amen.

Prayer for the World's Salvation

I stand before you, Merciful Lord,
    perturbed and tense.
I have no words.
My thoughts fly.
My heart beats in anguish.
I stand before you, Lord,
    to beg a very special blessing,
    not for me, but for all of us,
    for all humanity.
I stand before you, Lord,
    knowing human weakness,
    the darkness that reigns in all the corners of the world,
    the terrible sins of human beings,
    and the disregard of your divine laws.
I stand before you, Lord,
    fully aware of your great kindness,
    to beg your forgiveness
    for millions who have lost their way,
    asking for them salvation in this world.
I stand before you, Merciful Lord,
    now calmer than before, strong and sure again,
    with confidence in your mercy and kindness,
    asking for new opportunities, sure guidance,
    and more love,
    and for the salvation of this world.
Amen.

The Authors

Dr. Hugo Schlesinger is a freelance writer and journalist active in areas of economics, the arts, theater, cinema, and the promotion of fellowship and understanding between peoples of different nations, cultures, and religions. Dr. Schlesinger has actively participated in community life as a member of the Israel Culture Lodge, the Shalom Community of the Brazil-Israel Cultural Center, as founder of the magazine, *Heranca Judaica,* as chairman of the National Committee of Civil Rights and of B'nai B'rith, and as Chairman of Osvaldo Aranha Lodge for several terms.

Dr. Schlesinger holds doctorates in the fields of economics, social sciences, and philosophy. He was three times co-chairman of the Christian-Jewish Brotherhood Council. Dr. Schlesinger actively takes part in events concerning religious dialogue and as a Brazilian reporter has attended the Latin-American Meeting in Bogota, the International Meeting in New York, and the First Pan-American Congress for Catholic and Jewish Relationships. He is a member of the Nahinal Committee for the Dialogue between Catholics and Jews for the National Conference of Brazilian Bishops.

Among Dr. Schlesinger's many books are: *Who Killed Christ?, ABC of Jewish Thought, Jewish Roots of Christianity, The Gospels and the Jews.*

Rev. Humberto Porto is a Catholic priest of the Archdiocese of São Paulo in Brazil. He studied philosophy at the Central Seminary of Ipiranga and graduated in theology at the Pontifical Catholic University, both in São Paulo. Father Porto developed pastoral activities in his home town, including teaching, parochial service, and church group orientation. As sub-secretary of the National Secretarial for Vocations of the National Conference of Brazilian Bishops and editor of the vocational magazine, *Cadernos Vocacionais,* Father Porto has promoted vocational congresses and encounters at the national level.

Currently, Father Porto dedicated himself to the efforts of Christian-Jewish dialogue, having served three consecutive terms as President of the Christian-Jewish Fraternity Council. He is a member of the Catholic-Jewish National Dialogue Commission and of CEDRA

(Ecumenism and Religious Dialogue Commission of the Archdiocese of São Paulo). For the past twenty years, Father Porto has served as chaplain at the Colegio Nossa Senhora do Sion.

Among Father Porto's many books are: *Christian-Jewish Brotherhood* (2 volumes), *Christians and Jews, Jewish Worship and Christian Worship, The Teachings of the Second Vatican Council Concerning Jews.*

Index of Prayers

Achievement   57
Adoration   18
Bible   101
Birthday   13
Calm the spirit   68
Catastrophe victim   78
Children, in general   40
Children, one's own   36
City   86
Community   87
Contemplating nature   20
Creator   17
Courage   49
Culture, development of   89
Daily   8
Day of rest   11
Dead   75
Decision, before   59
Development of culture   89
Divine grace   54
Divine presence   21
Driver's   48
Doubt   24
Dying   74
Elderly   42
End of year   16
Evening   2
Executive's   46
Failure, after   62
Faith   50
Father   35
Fellowship   100
Festive day   12
Friends   98
Full life   23
Gift of life   33
God within   27
Goodness, work for   82
Grace, for divine   54
Guidance   31

Happiness   58
Harmony, international   90
Harvest time   83
Humanize life   84
Hungry   72
Husband's   37
Injustice victims   81
International harmony   90
Journey   9
Life, full   23
Life, meaning of   69
Life, thanks for   33
Life, to humanize   84
Loneliness   63
Love in deed   32
Meal, after   7
Meal, before   6
Meaning of life   69
Meeting, after   5
Meeting, before   4
Mental balance   66
Morning   1
Mother   34
Mourners   76
Nation, our   91
Nature, contemplating   20
Orphan   77
Patience   55
Peace   95
Physician's   45
Perseverance   26
Personal achievement   57
Poor   71
Praise   19
Pregnant woman's   39
Presence, divine   21
Prisoners   80
Progress of science   88
Protection   52
Refugees   79

Religious dialogue   102
Religious leaders   94
Repentance   64
Resist violence   65
Rulers   93
Salvation, world   104
Science, progress of   92
Security   96
Seeking God   99
Sharing   73
Sick   43
Sick person's   28
Signs of God   28
Silent moment   22
Sincere life   60
Spiritual concentration   30
Spirit, to calm one's   68
Spread of truth   85
Start of year   14
Success, after   61

Suffering   70
Teacher's   44
Test, before   67
Thanksgiving   53
Time, to use well   56
Truth, spread of   85
Unity   97
Uprightness   29
Vacation   10
Victims, of injustice   81
Violence, to resist   65
Wife's   38
Work, before   3
Work, for goodness   82
Worker's   47
World's salvation   104
Year, end of   16
Year, start of   14
Youngsters   41